Traditional Songs of Singing Cultures:

A WORLD SAMPLER

by Patricia Shehan Campbell, Sue Williamson, Pierre Perron

*The authors have donated their royalties to the
International Society for Music Education Organization.*

Editor: DEBBIE CAVALIER
Cover Design: FRANK MILONE & DEBBIE LIPTON
Book Layout: THAIS YANES

© 1996 WARNER BROS. PUBLICATIONS
All Rights Reserved

Any duplication, adaptation or arrangement of the compositions
contained in this collection requires the written consent of the Publisher.
No part of this book may be photocopied or reproduced in any way without permission.
Unauthorized uses are an infringement of the U.S. Copyright Act and are punishable by law.

Foreward

Because this project was developed under the auspices of the International Society for Music Education, preferatory remarks of the leadership comprise the foreward to the collection.

From Ana Lucia Frega, Buenos Aires, Argentina, ISME President 1996-1998:

A whole history of humanity could most fairly be named "the homo canens," the singerman (or woman). Love and sorrow, fear and joy, prayer and worship: all these meanings and messages are conveyed by pitches and timbres, voices and instruments. Let children of the world follow the magnificent path of songs from different continents and cultures. Let them be another moment in the history of "the homo canens." This collection of songs will help.

From Yasuharu Takahagi, Tokyo, Japan, ISME President 1992-1994:

The UNESCO constitution declared that "Since wars begin in the minds of men (and women), it is in the minds of men that the defense of peace must be constructed." It is to be lamented that international conflicts of various kinds have increased today. In such situations, music has the potential to play a major role in mutual understanding and a sensitivity towards other cultures within a framework of maintaining ethnic identities. Therefore, I hope that music education will be promoted throughout the world, in accordance with the spirit of the 1974 UNESCO recommendations regarding "Education for Human Rights, Fundamental Freedom and Education for International Understanding, Cooperation, and Peace." My wish is that the songs within this collection will be used by music teachers throughout the world, in the spirit of peace.

Dedication

To children everywhere who, like the songbirds of the forests,
have the natural capacity to sing, and to the teachers who take the time to
further their musical talents.

Acknowledgement

We are grateful for the expertise of sound engineer
Gary Louie of the University of Washington,
who gave extensively of his time to master the field tapes of this collection.

Contents

CD TRACK   **COUNTRY/CULTURE**   **SONG TITLE**   **PAGE**

Introduction

While music may not be a universal language, it is nonetheless an international phenomenon. People sing for every reason under the sun: to celebrate and to mourn, to express great love and joy, melancholy, and deep sorrow. They sing alone and together, as peaceful meditation and reflection or as a means of sharing a song's sentiments with family and friends. Even as technology mediates the songs of professional singers to any and all within listening range, adults and children are still singing. Everywhere in the world, songs are important avenues through which ideas and feelings are channeled. Songs and the act of singing appear to be a human constant, a distinctive means of expressing both ideas and feelings.

The songs featured within these pages are the result of a first gathering of songs from musician-teachers and friends of the International Society for Music Education. These songs are those that they know well from their own childhoods, and which they now offer to children and young students in the teaching they do. These teachers are preservers and transmitters of their own cultural heritages, as the songs they sing are expressive of not only musical features (melodies, rhythms, and timbres) deemed important by a cultural group, but also of the cultural values that are embedded in the songs' texts and functions. They consider the songs they have shared here as typical and representative of their musical and cultural heritage, and as a means of conveying to others some of the essence of both their personal and cultural preferences in the teaching of heritage songs to their students.

This collection features twenty songs from thirteen countries. While the world of song is not fully represesed in this first volume, there is nonetheless an assortment of world regions and cultures contained within: Africa (Eritrea and Uganda), Europe (Austria, England, France, Germany, Hungary, the Netherlands, and Portugal), Latin America (Argentina and Brazil), the Carribean (Barbados), Asia (Korea and Taiwan), the Pacific (New Zealand's Maori culture), and the United States. These songs are presented in standard western staff notation, but the real key to knowing the musical and linguistic essence of the songs is in listening to the accompanying CD. They are performed by "the culture-bearer," the musician-teacher whose first language (and musical language) is that of his or her selected song(s). Thus, these songs are made more real when listening to native-singers—tradition-bearers who know well their music and have been singing these songs for many years as children and teachers of children in their own culture.

The organization of the book is designed to proceed from one musical culture to the next, alphabetically. A brief introduction to the country or culture sets a frame of reference for the song. This is followed by the song itself—its notation and translation. Suggestions for the classroom use of the song are provided, including movement, game-related activities, and recommendations for the conceptual understanding of both musical and cultural features. A brief bibliography of English-language materials are suggested as well.

The songs contained herein may be seen as seeds for the development of a young singer's fuller understanding of music as an international phenomenon. Their performance and study leads also to an awareness of the meaning and value of these songs to their singing cultures. For what greater gift can a teacher give than songs that can take root and grow into the life of each of her students? Once sampled, these songs are likely to be sung again and again. They are the beautiful expressions of musical people who pass on their musical heritage to those of us eager to know the world a bit better.

Patricia Shehan Campbell
Sue Williamson
Pierre Perron

Notes on the Use of This Collection

The intent of this book and recording is to provide both songs and cultural information principally to teachers, parents, and childcare workers. The recording is central to learning the twenty songs, which are various in both language and musical style. By listening repeatedly with attention to the nuances of language, music, and vocal quality, these songs will begin to "roll off the tongue." The songs were selected for their "representativeness" of children's and/or traditional cultures. The brief descriptions of the countries and cultures from which the songs originate are intended as backdrop to the songs, and can be utilized as preliminary or follow-up information to actual experiences in listening and performing.

Those who use these songs may wish to include some of the following procedures, in order that children may be enriched both musically and culturally. Notice that some of these steps are preparatory to actual classroom use, so that instruction can proceed smoothly and with clear direction.

Prior to teaching the song:

1. Play the recording many times in order to become familiar (and confident) in singing the song.
2. Read the brief cultural description, highlighting or taking notes on some of the principal items and issues that identify the culture.
3. Locate the country on a globe or large map of the world or region.
4. Review magazines and newspapers, for colorful photographs of the country and its people to convert to color transparencies or prepare as bulletin board postings.
5. Try out some of the suggested activities (games, movements, instrumental accompaniments).

In the actual teaching of the songs to children:

1. Sing the song (live!) so that the children can know your own musical commitment to it.
2. Play the recording so that the children can hear the culture-bearer's own interpretation of the song.
3. Consider an immersion process, whereby children hear the whole song many times through, and begin singing as they become ready; break the song into "chunks" or phrases when words, pitches, or rhythms require it.
4. Utilize maps and photographs to provide a fuller cultural experience.
5. Discuss the function of the song and the meaning of the text. Extract words or phrases to be spoken and used in conversation.
6. Add suggested activities, but remind children of the importance of singing the song in order that the game or movement has its musical accompaniment.

Teachers vary in their purposes and goals of instructional material. While music teachers may hope to teach knowledge and skill in hearing, performing, reading and writing a particular melodic or rhythmic pattern, classroom teachers may utilize a song for its ability to express language or to present a cultural custom. Social science teachers may wish to emphasize the geographic location and ethnic-cultural composite of the country from which a song is derived, while physical education teachers may be attracted to a song's possibilities for movement and dance. These songs may invite all of these views—and more. A world of possibilities may exist for the instructional use of this collection, limited only by the creativity of the teachers.

Argentina

Cultural Information

Argentina occupies most of the southern portion of the South American continent, with an extensive Atlantic coastline. Once largely a producer of livestock and agricultural goods, Argentina is now highly industrialized and is currently one of the world's principal trading nations. Still, its four topographical regions—the central flat and fertile *pampas*, the forested plains to the northeast, the Andean mountains to the west, and the arid and windy plateaus of the southern Patagonia—offer images of colorful *gauche* (cowboy), farmers, and rugged frontier people that have contributed richly to Argentina's history.

Descendants of sixteenth-century Spanish settlers and nineteenth-century Italian immigrants comprise nearly three-quarters of the population. Other Western European Argentineans, whose ancestors arrived from France, Germany, the United Kingdom, Switzerland, and Portugal, account for almost ten percent; eight percent of the population are Eastern European Argentineans (including Poles, Russians, Hungarians, Turks, and South Slavs). Argentina's Jewish population is the largest in Latin America. While Native American Indians are almost completely absorbed into the general population, almost ten percent of Argentineans are *mestizo*—of mixed Indian and European ancestry.

Aside from the vibrant symphonic, choral, and opera scenes (particularly in Buenos Aires) where works by European and Argentinean national composers such as Alberto Ginastera are performed, there are rich traditions of Argentinean indigenous, and mestizo and Creole music, that are performed, preserved, and dynamically changing. Although only 30,000 Native American Indians survive, their ceremonial and seasonal musics are present in various forms from Andean communities near the northwestern border with Bolivia, to groups living as far south as Patagonia. Creole entertainment songs, Carnival songs, and dance songs are predominantly European in nature, and may feature guitars, *charangos* (five-stringed armadillo-backed lutes, near Bolivia), harp, accordion, and *bomba* (bass barrel drum). The lively *cueca* dance can be found in western Argentina, and the *tango*, the national dance, can be found in its original urban style and in rural recreational style. Common children's singing games are often European in origin, including *Arroz con leche, Hilito de oro, Sobre el puente de Avinon* [see France, Sur le Pont d'Avignon], and *La torre en guardia.*

About the Song : ¿Quien es ese Pajarito?

"¿Quien es ese Pajarito?" is an Argentinean *chaya*, a song to be danced in free movements. Maria Carmen del Aguilar remembers learning it from a radio program in Buenos Aires in the late 1950s. At 13, she listened to the many popular artists from the northern provinces of Argentina, and would "figure out" the guitar accompaniments by ear. Much later, this early exposure to folk music led to her own scholarly research of the music.

Some chayas, like this one, use the minor pentatonic scale in their melody, although they are accompanied by the minor-mode normal harmony which includes sounds that "don't belong" in the pentatonic scale. They are often sung to the accompaniment of guitar or charango. Percussion instruments add to the flavor of chayas including the caja or bombo and a set of goat's hooves that are shaken together.

Teaching Suggestions and Extensions

1. While listening, perform several movements to reinforce the triple meter of the song. Begin with a patsch on the lap for beat one, adding on beats two and three the small movement of the hand in the shape of the beak of a talking bird.

    patsch   bird   bird
                   beak   beak

2. Add a drum for each beat, using a soft mallet on hand drum or timpani. Rattles can be shaken on the beat, or randomly.

3. A guitar accompaniment can be added, utilizing F, C, and Am in a strum featuring quarter-notes or a  (down, down-up, down-up) rhythm.

4. Ask children to consider what type of little bird is singing in the tree, naming small birds they know. As an extension, assign children the task of preparing a report on birds native to their home (and to Argentina, or more generally, to South America).

¿Quien es ese pajarito?

(Who is that little bird?)

Translation by
Maria Carmen del Aguilar

Traditional

1. ¿Quien es e - se pa - ja - ri - to
2. Si me qui - er - es con - o - cer,

que can - ta so - bre el li - mon? _____ An - da y
pa - sa - te por el jar - din _____ Al - li es -

di - le _____ que no can - te _____ que me
ta mi _____ nom - bre e - scri - to _____ en la

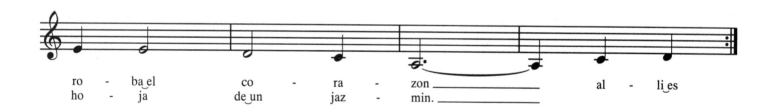

ro - ba el co - ra - zon _____ al - li es
ho - ja de un jaz - min. _____

Translation

1. Who is that little bird
   That sings over the lemon tree?
   Go and tell him to stop singing
   Because he is stealing my heart.

2. If you want to know me better,
   Come along my garden.
   There is my name written
   On the leaf of a jasmine plant.

Austria

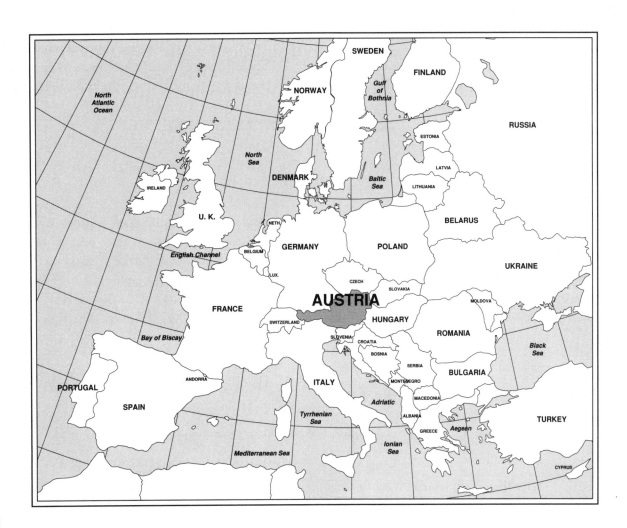

 ## Cultural Information

Bordered by eight countries, Austria is a landlocked republic in Central Europe. Its historical and cultural ties to Germany are long-standing (it was named "Oesterrich"—eastern state—by the Germans in the tenth century). Other ethnic peoples, including the Magyars of Hungary, the Slavs, and the Latins, also influenced its cultural development. About a third of its population live in cities like Vienna, Innsbruck, and Salzburg, while the remainder live in small towns and in the increasingly developed Alpine region. Most Austrians speak German and practice Roman Catholicism, although minority populations of Croats and Slovenes, and smaller populations of Hungarians, Czechs, Slovaks, Italians, and Jews also reside there. Despite the "tugs of war" it has known in its political history over the last century, including its principal role as part of the vast Austro-Hungarian Empire prior to World War I, it has reclaimed today its former image of upland valleys, farming communities, and colorful mountain villages.

While Vienna is recognized as one of the leading cities of Western European art music, and Salzburg has become symbolic of Mozart festivals, *The Sound of Music*, and studies in Orff-Schulwerk, Austrians also know distinctive folk music traditions that vary from one province to the next. Two musical forms that are best known are the *jodler* (yodel) and the *landler* (a dance in triple time). The jodler is typically a melody in a major key and triple meter, which includes both a verse and a wordless yodeled refrain that rapidly alternates between chest and head registers. The rich mountainous region of the Tyrol is a repository even today of jodlers, and of landlers played on fiddles, button-key accordions, string bass, and the rare wooden-keyed xylophones.

Austrian folk music is frequently set in triple meter, and features triadic and stepwise melodies in major keys. When instruments and voices play together, the result is often a rich homophony (melody with choral accompaniment). Anacrusic phrase structures are commonly found, and also melodies flavored with dotted rhythms. Seasonal carols at Christmas (including *Stille Nacht* [Silent Night] and *Kommen der Kinder* [Come, Little Children]) and Easter narrative songs and dance songs are among the traditional genres still preserved in performances today.

 ## About the Song: Kommt Ein Vogel Geflogen

"Kommt Ein Vogel Geflogen" is an Austrian folk song which Anne Peschek learned from her Austrian husband. When he was only two years old, his mother would sing this song for him—and eventually with him. In many cultures, the first songs of childhood are about birds or animals, and "things" close to home. Anne's husband remembers singing the song with his siblings and cousins at family gatherings in Austria. While there is only the even rhythm of quarter—and eighth-note patterns, the anacrusis that begins each two-measure phrase, along with triple meter and triadic melody, make for the distinctive Austrian sound.

 ## Teaching Suggestions and Extensions

1. Practice singing the mi-fa-sol (mm. 1, 5, 9, 13) and re-mi-fa (mm. 3, 7, 11, and 15) patterns, which move rather quickly in ♫ ♩ anacrusic rhythms. Then, sing the song, asking children to raise their right hands on mi-fa-sol and their left hands on re-mi-fa, when these patterns occur.

2. Play the song on autoharp, in order to give a taste of the traditional Tyrolean plucked zither. Tonic (F) and dominant (C7) chords are sufficient, in a strum that features the low strings on beat one, and two higher and lighter strums for beats two and three.

3. Extend to a singing game. Children sit in a circle, while one child is chosen to act as a bird who carries a letter (perhaps an empty envelope). As children sit and sing with their hands behind their backs, the bird flies around the outside of the circle, dropping the letter into the hands of one child who will become the next bird.

4. Ask children to create a list of familiar songs about birds (include "¿Quien es ese Pajarito?").

Kommt ein Vogel Geflogen

Translation by
Ann Peschek

Traditional

Kommt ein Vo - gel ge - flo - gen, setst sich nie - der auf mein'

Fuss, hat's ein Brief - chen im Schna - bel, von der Mut - ter ei - nen

Gruss, Lie - ber Vo - gel, fling' wei - ter, bring ein Gruss mit, ei - nen

Kuss, denn ich kann dich nicht be - glei - ten, weil ich hier blei - ben muss.

Translation
A Bird flies to me and lights on my foot.
He has a letter in his beak, and greetings from my mother.
Dear little bird, fly and take a greeting and a kiss.
I cannot go with you now, for I must stay here.

Barbados

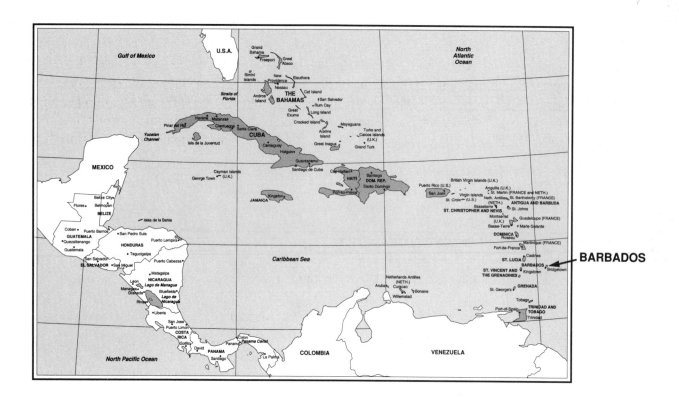

Cultural Information

Situated over 200 miles north of the coast of Venezuela, Barbados is the easternmost country of the islands of the West Indies. Barbados is known for its warm and pleasant climate, moderate temperatures, and sunny beaches. It is a densely populated country, and nearly 90% of its people are descendants of Africans who were settled there as slaves nearly three centuries ago.

The British colonized Barbados, beginning in 1627. African slaves were brought to the island to work the sugar cane fields. Although the importation of slaves was abolished by the British Empire in 1834, British dominance of labor and land usage continued for over a century longer. Black workers rallied for their political and civil rights, and for their ultimate independence from England in 1966. Legacies of the British rule are yet found in the choice of "the King's English" as the official language, and in the popularity of Christian Protestant worship practices. The island beckons tourists from the colder climates, and exports much of its tropical produce, including sugar and bananas.

Like the West Indian culture at large, music in Barbados is a syncretic blend of African and European elements. The European scales are often combined with African call-and-response forms, and with rhythmic hand-clapping accompaniments. Like many forms of Afro-Caribbean music, the music of Barbados is often "fit for dancing," and is marked by drumming on single-and double-headed drums, and by bamboo tubes that are stamped on the ground. Many singing games are preserved by children in Barbados, some utilizing English melodies, but seasoned with syncopations and local dialects.

About the Song: Pack She Back to She Ma

"Pack She Back to She Ma" is a well-known song in Barbados, with variants found in a number of Caribbean cultures. When Janice Millington-Robertson was just five years old, she learned the song from her parents and sang it as well in school. It is a popular song at informal gatherings and at folk festivals, and is often the song a Barbadian sings spontaneously when asked to share something of the musical culture of her island-country. While more of a "joke" today, the song is a reminder of the domestic obligations traditionally expected of a married woman in her new home; when these social responsibilities were not met, there was the chance that the woman could be sent by her husband back to her family home - quite possibly to learn to wash and cook!

Teaching Suggestions and Extensions

1. Try the following movements while singing the song:

MM 1 - 4   Throw right hand out in front (a vigorous thrust) then left hand, as if sending someone annoying away.

MM 5 - 6   Hands akimbo on both sides, with right foot forward and separated from left foot.

"The girl wouldn't wash"
   Make a motion as in the washing clothes by hand.

"The girl wouldn't cook"
   Make a motion as in stirring a pot by hand

2. Perform this movement for the phrase, "Pack she back to she ma."

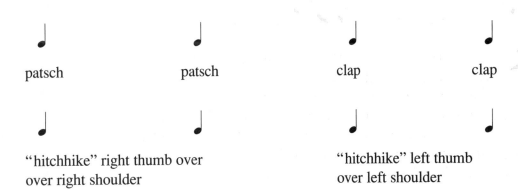

3. Discuss and demonstrate changes of phrase, from Barbadian dialect to "the King's English." What words might be substituted?
   Answers may include:
   "pack she back to she ma" = "send her back to her mother"
   "she lazy 'til she born" = "she was lazy since she was born"

Pack She Back to She Ma

Translation by
Janice Millington Robertson

Traditional

Pack she back to she ma oh! Pack she back to she ma. What a

pret-ty lit-tle girl like Jes-sie Ma-hone, pack she back to she ma.

pack she back to she ma. With a pret-ty lit-tle girl like Jes-sie Ma-hone, she

la - zy 'til she born ____ the girl would-n't wash, the girl would-n't cook, so I

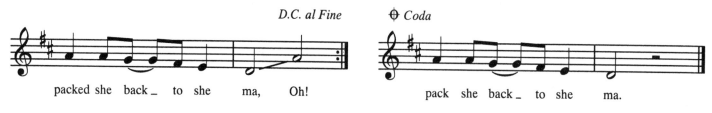

packed she back to she ma, Oh!   pack she back to she ma.

Brazil

Cultural Information

The largest country in South America goes by its official name, "The Federative Republic of Brazil." Stretching from the Andes Mountains eastward to the Atlantic Ocean, Brazil occupies almost half of the geographic region of South America (and is the world's fifth largest country in area). Most Brazilians live in the densely populated area of eastern Brazil, in cities like Sao Paulo, Rio de Janeiro, Salvador, and Recife. Many rural peoples have migrated to the cities, and have taken residence in *favelas,* or shantytowns, on the edges of the urban areas.

Brazil's rich ethnic and cultural diversity is reflected in its history. Besides the indigenous peoples, the Portuguese began to colonize there in the sixteenth century, and from 1538-1888 (three hundred and fifty years), almost five million African slaves were brought to Brazil from Angola, the Congo, Nigeria, and Dahomey. While it is a heterogeneous population today, most Brazilian citizens are united by language: Brazil is the largest Portuguese-speaking country in the world. Over 90 percent of Brazil's population claims Catholicism as their religious preference, although many practice folk religions that combine Catholic and African elements in theology and worship practices.

The rich ethnic diversity of Brazil is also reflected in its arts and music. Folk arts and crafts thrive in the rural areas, and many painters use rural people as subjects for artistic expression. Brazil's music is a syncretic blend of Portuguese, African, and indigenous influences. Portuguese influence is noted in the cycles of folk festivals which blend secular and sacred characters. Music and dance are important elements of the festival celebrations, including Fest do Divino (Feasts of the Divine Being), winter and summer solstices, and Carnaval. Rio's Carnaval, a famous festival held before Lent, is a festive showcase of the samba which displays African origins. African influences are also reflected in the use of flat seventh scale degrees, hemiola rhythms (meters that move between 3/4 and 6/8), and call-and-response singing. The influence of the indigenous traditions is notable in the use of maracas and certain choreographic gestures and genres.

About the Song: Pirulito

"Pirulito" is a popular children's song in Brazil. Ilza Zenker Leme Joly has sweet memories of the song from her earliest childhood. She learned it from her mother when she was just two years old, and sang it with friends and schoolmates. Even today, the song can be heard by children playing in the street or taking a recess from their studies at school. Ilza notes that "Even now, I always use the song in my music classes."

The rhythm of "Pirulito" is catchy and typically Brazilian in character, and the lyrics reflect the sad reality of loving and losing someone very dear. A hand-clapping game provides further rhythmic interest in the performance of the song.

Teaching Suggestions and Extensions

1. Using the "body scale," lead children in singing from high to low (doh to doh, or 8 to 1). Follow these gestures, one to a pitch:

doh	8	hands on top of head
ti	7	hands on ears
la	6	hands on shoulders
sol	5	hands held out in front, waist high, palms up
fa	4	hands on waist
mi	3	hands on lap (mid-thigh)
re	2	hands on knees
doh	1	hands on ankles (or feet)

2. Sing the song, using the gestures of the "body scale" for the two repetitions of the descending major scale (MM. 6-7-8; 14-15-16).

3. Clap the typical Brazilian rhythm: ♩ ♩ ♩ each time it occurs in the song.

   Play the extended rhythm ♩ ♩ ♩ ♩ as an ostinato, on claves, conga drums, and maracas.

4. Once children know the song well, challenge to create a handclapping pattern of their own to perform with a partner.

Pirulito

Translation by
Ilza Zenker Leme Joly

Traditional

Pi - ru - li - to que ba - te ba - te Pi - ru - li - to que já ba -

teu. Quem gos - ta de mim é e - la, quem gos - ta de - la sou

eu. Pi - ru - li - to que ba - te ba - te Pi - ru - li - to que já ba -

teu. A me - ni - na q'eu a - ma - va coi - ta - di - nha ja mor - reu.

Translation
Lollipop that beats and beats
Lollipop that has already beaten.
She's the one who loves me
I'm the one who loves her.

Lollipop that beats and beats
Lollipop that has already beaten.
The girl who I loved,
Poor one! She has already died . . .

Canada

Cultural Information

Canada takes its name from the Huron-Iroquois nation's *Kanata*, a word meaning village or community. In area, Canada is the second largest country in the world. It is bordered on three sides by oceans (the Atlantic, the Pacific, and the Arctic), with the United States on its southern side. Most Canadians live in the southern third of the country, leaving about 90 percent of it nearly unsettled, thus accounting for one of the lowest population densities in the world. Cities like Montreal, Toronto, and Vancouver, however, blend historic sites with high technology, and boast ideal living conditions.

Officially, Canada has a bicultural heritage, with strong connections to England and France. Historically, this cultural marriage was brought on by the British conquest of New France in 1763. Today, both English and French are official languages in Canada. French Canadians now account for 27% of the population, living mostly in the eastern provinces of Quebec and New Brunswick. Indigenous people, including Athabascan and Coast Salish Indians in the western and northern provinces and Alkgonkian and Iroquoian Indians of the eastern woodlands, comprise the oldest strata of the population. Sizable communities of Scandinavians exist in the central provinces of Saskatchewan and Manitoba, with Celtic peoples (Irish and Scotch) living in the far eastern provinces of Nova Scotia, Newfoundland, Labrador, and Prince Edward's Island. Immigrants from eastern European and Middle Eastern countries have settled in Ontario, principally in Toronto. Canadian arts reflect most prominently the heritages of the British, French, and Canadian Indians. There are four major orchestras in Canada, four major opera companies, and three professional ballet companies, along with numerous community ensembles of singers and players. Canadian Indian music is largely vocal, although whistles, drums and rattles of a wide variety of types may be used to define rhythm and mood. Most French-Canadian songs can be traced to northern France, although they were brought by immigrants between 1664-72, and some date to the unaccompanied song of the Medieval troubadours. Fiddles are still played for dances in a style that blends both French and Celtic elements. The British musical heritage is evident in the ballads that are sung, and in the English country dancing accompanied by a variety of stringed instruments.

About the Song: Ah! Si Mon Moine Voulait Danser!

When Pierre Perron was just a young boy in Montreal, Quebec, "Ah! Si Mon Moine Voulait Danser!" was one of the songs his mother sang to him. The song refers to a monk with whom the singer hopes to dance, for which he would give him his belt, rosary, home-spun frock, or other treasures. The song was a favorite of the Acadians, a cultural group living on the south shore of the St. Lawrence River. When they were expelled by the British in 1755, they took their language and culture, including this song with them to the bayou country of Louisiana in the southern United States. This song is preserved not only in eastern Canada but also by the Cajuns of Louisiana.

Teaching Suggestions and Extensions

1. Sing the song lightly, while patsching the rhythm of the words on the lap. On cue, patsch only while singing silently, returning again to sing the melody on another cue.

2. Step the rhythm of the French-Canadian step-dance, sitting or standing, while singing.

3. Play the step-dance rhythm on spoons to accompany the song. Use metal or wooden kitchen spoons, or "musical spoons" already attached for ease in holding and playing.

4. Examine a map of North America, referring to the French Canadian province of Quebec, the St. Lawrence River region of the Acadians, and the Cajun country of southern Louisiana (U.S.).

Ah! Si Mon Moine Voulait Danser!

Translation by
Pierre Perron

Traditional

Verse:

1. Ah! si mon moi - ne vou - lait dan - ser! Ah! si mon moi - ne vou - lait dan - ser! Un

ca - pu - chon je lui don - ne - rais, Un ca - pu - chon je lui don - ne - rais.

Refrain:

Dan - se, mon moin', dan - se, Tu n'en - tends pas la dan - se, Tu

n'en - tends pas mon mou - lin lon la, Tu n'en - tends pas mon mou - lin mar - cher.

Verses
2. Un ceinturon
3. Un chapelet
4. Un froc de bur'
5. Un beau psautier
6. S'il n'avait fait voeu de pauvrete,
   Bien d'autres chos's je lui donnerais.

Translation
Verse
1. Oh! If only my monk would dance with me,
   A hooded robe I'd give him free.

Refrain: Dance, my monk, dance.
   You don't hear the dance.
   You don't hear my little windmill there.
   You don't hear my windmill work.

2. A braided belt
3. A rosary
4. A home-spun frock
5. A prayer book (book of psalms)
6. Oh! If he hadn't made a vow of poverty,
   Many more things I would give him.

England

 ## Cultural Information

The largest of the countries that comprise the "United Kingdom," England occupies the south part of the island of Great Britain. Along with Scotland and Wales, this island is off the northeastern coast of the European mainland. England's name is derived from the Angles, a Germanic people who invaded the island along with the Saxons in the fifth century. It is a country of lowlands in the south and central regions, and highlands in the north, with a climate of cool summers and mild winters.

England is densely populated, with 90% of the population living in urban areas; London's population exceeds seven million. Along with the Anglo-Saxon descendants live large numbers of recent Commonwealth immigrants: Scots, Welsh, Irish; Indians and Pakistani who number about 4%; and various African and Caribbean people who were once colonized by the British.

While the subject of music in England may conjure up aural images of Purcell, Elgar, Vaughn Williams, Walton, Britten, and Tippett, there is also a rich legacy of folksong and dance music that is nurtured through festivals and "sessions" of singers, instrumentalists, and dancers who gather regularly. An English folksong is generally syllabic, of four-line stanzas, in duple, triple, and 6/8 time, often with "conceits" or stock phrases like "As I walked out" and "My own true love." Melodies of six pitches (without the 3rd, 6th, or 7th degree) are most frequently in a major mode, although mixolydian, dorian, and aeolian melodies are found in large numbers. Systematic collections of English folksongs date to the work of Bishop Percy in 1765, although the centerpiece collection of 3,000 tunes (including variants) by Cecil Sharp from 1903 to 1924 is the greatest treasure. Children's singing games, many of which have been collected and analyzed by Peter and Iona Opie, combine singing, gestures, and dancing. Within these songs are often embedded aspects of England's ancient customs.

About the Song: Billy Boy

As Kathy Anderson explained the text, "It's like a mother talking to a son, asking if this girl is good enough to be his wife." The song moves rhythmically in compound meter, skipping lightly, and utilizing the full diatonic scale. It substitutes "me" for "my," demonstrating some of the dialect from its rustic origins, and often excludes the final "g" from such words as "walkin(g)" and "charmin(g)." While other melodies are known for a similar text about "Billy Boy," this one is lively, contagious, and very English.

Teaching Suggestions and Extensions

1. While singing the song, keep the pulse. Then, keep the "skip-ty" rhythm: ♩ ♪.
   Finally, keep the rhythm of "Billy boy": ♩ ♪♩.

2. Play the melody on recorder and add a hand drum on the "skip-ty" rhythm, thus giving the flavor of an old English one-person pipe and drum sound.

3. Seek out variants of the song. The Anglo-American "Where Have You Been, Billy Boy?" is one of them. Compare and contrast their the texts, rhythms, and melodies of the two songs.

Billy Boy

Traditional

Where have ye been all the day?
Is she fit to be your wife? Bil - ly Boy, Bil - ly Boy. Is she
Can she cook an I - rish stew?

ye been all the day?
fit to be your wife me Bil - ly Boy? She's a fit to be me wife as the
cook an I - rish stew? She can cook an I - rish stew eye and

char - min' Nan - cy Gray.
fork is to the knife and me Nan - cy Kit - tle - me - fan - cy. Oh, me char - min' Bil - ly Boy. __
sing in Hin - nies too,

Eritrea

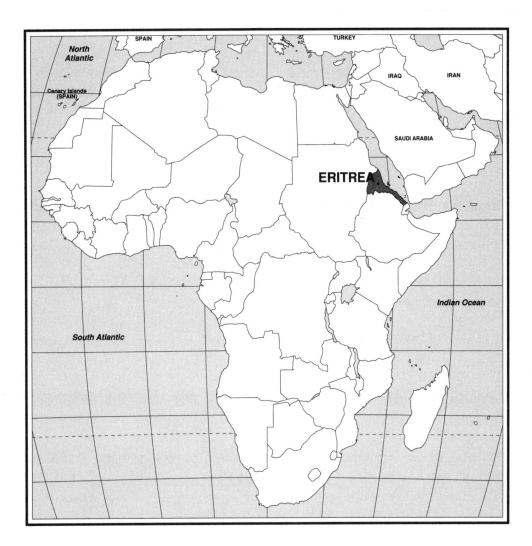

 ## Cultural Information

Located in northeastern Africa, the recently independent country of Eritrea borders the Red Sea in the east, Sudan in the west and north, and Ethiopia in the south. Its new independence came in 1993 after nearly thirty years of civil war with Ethiopia. Eritrea is a mountainous country which displays varying topography between the highlands (which reach nearly 7,000 feet) and the surrounding sea-level lowlands.

Eritrea's population are almost equally divided in their religious beliefs and practices, between Ethiopian Orthodox Christians and Muslims. One of many languages is Tigrinya, of Semitic origin; Afar, Beni, Amer, Tigre, and Arabic are also spoken. Many of the people are involved with livestock and agriculture, with highlanders tending to farming and nomadic lowlanders tending to goats and camels.

For Eritreans, music is integral to life. Singing begins very early, and is continuous—at play, work, for weddings, births, and funerals. Instrumental accompaniment is not necessary, although the *kirar* (a five-string lute) and *keboro* (a two-headed drum) may occasionally be added. Hand-clapping is the most typical accompaniment, while gestures and movement patterns are also common practices while singing.

About the Song: Meseraseri

"Meseraseri" is a lullaby sung by mothers to their infants. The language of the song is Tigrinya, and as the translation indicates, the poetic images serve to praise all the best assets of the baby boy or girl. The phrase, "you command like a lion in the wild," certainly brings emphasis to the masculine nature of boys, just as "pretty as flowers" addresses the femininity of girls. "Nwedi" refers to the verses particular to boy infants, and "ngual" refers to verses for girl infants.

The pentatonic melody is chanted, with breaths in between phrases that vary in metric shape, from 5/4 to 4/4 to 2/4. The poetry is the principal element in the chant, thus directing the melody into its changing meters. As Hidaat Ephrem noted, "This song is unnatural, if not sung with the movements of bouncing a child on the lap." The movement thus reinforces the melody, the rhythm, and the poetry.

 Teaching Suggestions and Extensions

1. Sing the individual phrases repeatedly, and determine the number of pulses (the meter) of each phrase.

2. With dolls and stuffed animals on children's laps, sing the song, bouncing them in time to the pulse.

3. Recall other familiar lullabies. Does "Meseraseri" meet the criteria of a lullaby? How should it be sung?

4. Locate Eritrea on a map (an older map will erroneously include the present-day Eritrea as the northern region of Ethiopia). Discuss the cultural influences of countries situated in "crossroads" regions of the world. While Eritrea is located on the African continent, it retains influences of its northern neighbors in the Middle East. (A similar "crossroads" culture is Thailand, which knows both Chinese and Indian influences.)

Meseraseri

Translation by
Hidaat Ephrem

Traditional

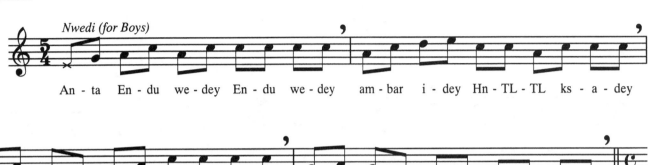

Nwedi (for Boys)

An - ta En - du we - dey En - du we - dey am - bar i - dey Hn - TL - TL ks - a - dey

k - mel - se - ka do - mo nab - za keb - dey k - mel - se - ka do - mo - nab - za keb - dey.

En - du we - dey En - du we - dey an - be - sa be - re - ka me - kau E - de - di

qe - cha A - ter me - Se beg me - a - di En - du we - dey

En - du we - dey K - mel - se - ka do - mo nab - za keb dey.

Ngual (for Girls)

Hn - Tit gua - ley Hn - Tit gua - ley Am - bar i - dey Hn - TL TL - k - sa - dey

K - mel - se - ka do - mo - nab - za keb - dey k - mel - se - ka do - mo nab - za keb - dey

re - ey wi - El - ka - ya ze yt - m - no zey y - S - geb en Je - a I - ma - no

n - A - Ki - fe Ti - ru z - y - Ko - no Hn - Tit gua - ley

Hn - Tit gua - ley k - mel - se - ka do - mo nab - za keb - dey.

Translation
My baby boy, by baby boy
You make me look good
Like a handsome bracelet on my wrists
Like the jewels on my neck
Should I start all over again
From conception to birth?
You are such a delight.

My baby boy, My baby boy
You command like a lion in the wild
Your presence graces me like a tasty bread
That decorates a feastful table
Should I start all over again
From conception to birth?
You are such a delight.

My baby girl, my baby girl
You make me look good
Like a handsome bracelet on my wrists
Like the jewels on my neck
Should I start all over again
From conception to birth?
You are such a delight.

My baby girl, my baby girl
Pretty as flowers
I could look at you all day
And never get tired of it
You are like a sampler food
That is too delicious and too little
The gods should have stopped after creating you
My baby girl, my baby girl
Should I start all over again
From conception to birth?
You are such a delight.

France

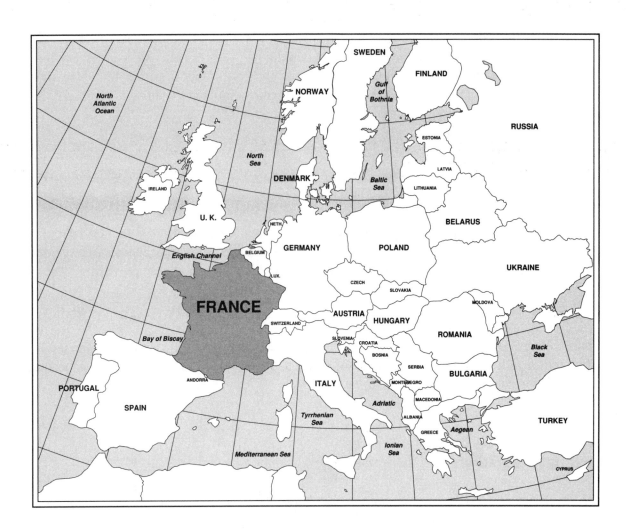

 ## Cultural Information

Derived from the Latin "Francia" (meaning "country of Franks"), France is the largest country in Western Europe. Roughly shaped like a hexagon, three of its six sides are bordered by water: the English channel on the northwest, the Atlantic Ocean on the West, and the Mediterranean Sea on the southeast. The other sides border seven European countries: Belgium, Luxembourg, Germany, Switzerland, Italy, Spain, and Andorra. Four climactic types prevail in France, including a maritime climate in the west, a continental climate in the interior, a mountain climate, and a Mediterranean climate.

The French population is largely native-born, and is a blending of the Celtic, Germanic, Latin, and Slavic peoples. Twentieth-century immigrants number nearly four million, chief among them are the Portuguese, Spaniards, Italians, and Algerians. The traditional French culture remains stable and strong despite immigration, partly through the conscious effort to retain exclusive use of the French language in schools and society. France, and particularly Paris, is often considered the hallmark of Western aesthetics. France is home to the artistic movements of impressionism and cubism, and is a leader of the Western fashion design industry. It is also world-famous for its wine production.

The French have made distinctive marks in the realm of music. France claims many of the musical leaders of the impressionist movement of the late 19th century. Composers associated with French musical innovations of the 19th and 20th century include Faure, Debussy, Franck, Saint-Saens, Ravel, Poulenc, and Satie. Folk music in France continues to be quite popular, with instruments such as fiddles, flutes, hurdy-gurdy, bagpipes, the accordian, and the nasal timbre of Pyrenean (Basque) oboes commanding the attention of singers, dancers, and avid listeners. Popular and "world pop" music continues to gain audiences, but the old French folk songs are preserved through school programs and seasonal festivals.

About the Song: Sur le Pont d'Avignon

"Sur la Pont d'Avignon" is known to every French child before he or she enters school. It is an historic song that has survived many centuries, having been passed orally from one generation to the next. Alain Carre remembered that his first teacher at a preschool he attended taught him this song when he was just three years old. Each time he hears it, he is reminded of his own childhood.

The song is not a carrier of religious, political, or social beliefs (which can be the case of many children's songs—let alone folk songs). It simply tells of the bridge (or deck) at Avignon, a city in the southeastern region of Provence, located at the confluence of two rivers. This bridge has been the site for much dancing and merry-making through the ages.

Teaching Suggestions and Extensions

1. Ask children to name famous bridges they know—in their country, and in their neighborhood. Locate Avignon on a map of France, and the rivers over which the bridge was built.

2. Patsch the rhythm of the refrain's melody while singing, and then while singing silently. Note that the verse may be sung either freely (as on the recording) or in strict rhythm that distinguishes the triplet from the eighth-note couplet.

3. Once the song is known, dance the song. Children may form a circle, moving right to the pulse for the first eight measures. For measures 9-12 (a verse of sorts), the movements designated by the text can be performed (bow, curtsy, salute, gesture the playing of an instrument).

Sur le Pont d'Avignon

Translation by
Alain Carre

Traditional

Sur   le   pont   d'Av - ign - on,   on   y   dan - se,   on   y   dan - se,

sur   le   pont   d'Av - ign - on,   on   y   dan - se   tous   en   round.

Verse:

1. Les beaux mon-sieurs   font   comm'   ci,   Et   les bell's damm's font   comm'   ca.
2. Les mil - i - taires   font   comm'   ca.   Et   puis en - cor'   comm'   ca.
3. Les mus - i - ciens   font   comm'   ca.   Et   puis en - cor'   comm'   ca.

Translation

Refrain:
On the bridge of Avignon,
    Everyone dances, everyone dances,
    On the bridge of Avignon,
    Everyone dances in a round.

Verse:
1. The handsome gentlemen do this, (bow)
    And the beautiful ladies do that. (curtsy)
2. The soldiers do that, (salute)
    And then again, do that.
3. The musicians do that, (play an instrument)
    And then again, do that.

Germany

Cultural Information

Unified Germany is located in central Europe and borders Denmark to the north, Poland and the Czech Republic to the east, Austria and Switzerland to the south, and France, Luxembourg, Belgium and the Netherlands to the west. There is geographic variety in Germany, from the hilly northern lowlands to the Alpine forestlands of the south. People worldwide were drawn to their televisions in 1990 as they watched the physical removal of the bricks of the Berlin wall which had separated East and West Germany for 45 years; today Germany is a single political and economic union.

Religious and ethnic diversity is apparent in Germany. There is no state church, although Protestant and Roman Catholic churches and Jewish synagogues receive government support. Since the late 1980s, large numbers of immigrants from eastern Europe and Turkey have sought relief from religious, political, and economic oppression, and have settled there.

The music of Germany ranges from German polka bands at the Oktoberfests to the dramatic music of Richard Wagner. German folk music tends to contain diatonic melodies, often ascending, which frequently begin on the anacrusis, and includes tones that are repeated expressively. The complete picture of German folk includes styles as varied as those of Schwabia, Bavaria, and Westphalia, of peasants, miners, and journeymen, of ballads, carols, and the Alpine *schnadahupfl*. Throughout history, German folk music has been influenced by the changing styles of art music of the gentry and minstrels, as well as the surrounding European countries.

About the song: Alle Meine Entchen

"Alle Meine Entchen" is a children's song. Anne Peschek learned it from her husband, who in turn remembered hearing his mother sing it when he was just a toddler. He recalls the most attractive thing about the song was the chance to imitate the sounds of the ducks. It opens its melody in a quick ascending passage, repeats the sixth degree, and then falls again to the tonic—a typical melodic turn in German traditional music.

 ## Teaching Suggestions and Extensions

1. While singing the song, include this body percussion accompaniment for every two-measure phrase:

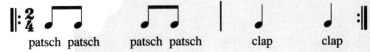

2. In a circle, hold hands while stepping lightly to the pulse. On the third phrase, drop hands and bend heads down low. On phrase four, raise bottoms up.

3. Ask children to recall songs and singing games that feature the sounds and movements of animals and birds.

Alle meine Entchen

Translation by
Anne Peschek

Traditional

Al - le mei - ne Ent - chen schwim-men auf dem See,

Kopf - chen in das Was - ser, Schwanz-chen in die Hoh.

Translation
All of the ducks swim on the lake,
Head in the water, tail up high.

Hungary

 ## Cultural Information

Hungary is located in Europe, and is coterminous with Austria and Slovenia in the west, Slovakia in the north, the Ukraine in the northeast, Romania in the east, and Croatia and Serbia in the south. In 1990, its government switched from a one-party communist state to a democratic government, which is resulting in the transformation of many sectors of society and government. Ethnically, Hungary is a rather homogenous nation. The largest ethnic group, the Magyars, constitute around ninety percent of the population. Other ethnic groups represented are Germans, Slovaks, South Slavs, Romanians, and Gypsies. There are also large numbers of Magyars living outside Hungary; more than two million live in Romania and Slovakia and about one million live in Western Europe, the United States, Canada, and elsewhere.

Hungary has produced numerous artists known internationally for their talents. Among them is the artist Laszlo Moholy-Nagy, architect Marcel Breder, and composers Franz Liszt, Bela Bartok, and Zoltan Kodaly. Famous Hungarian conductors have included Fritz Reiner, George Szell, Eugence Ormancy and Sir Georg Solti. The Hungarian "high arts" have been much influenced by the folk traditions found in the many rural communities throughout the country.

The importance of folk music is evident in both classical and non-classical genres of Hungarian music. Most notably, the composers Bartok and Kodaly built their musical reputations on collecting thousands of folksongs and later writing compositions based on the folk pieces. Bartok classified two main styles of Hungarian folksong, the "old" and the "new." Characteristics of the old style include the use of the anhemitonic pentatonic scale and a descending melodic structure in which the second half of the melody is often a fifth lower. A steady beat, *parlando* (free speech-like) rhythm, and moderate ornamentation are also common features. The main feature of the new style is the repetitive arched melodic structure. Children's melodies are most often built on a hexachord tonal system, are in duple time, and are repeated with slight variations according to the rhythmic syllables of the text. Instruments in the folk tradition include a combination of simple home-made instruments as well as those professionally marketed, including the reed-pipe, flute, bagpipe, wooden trumpet, *citera* (zither), *gombos harmonika* (button accordion), and the swineherd's cow horn.

About the Song: Ég a Gyertya

"Ég a Gyertya" is a children's singing game. Katalin Forrai learned this song from other children on the playground when she was about four years old. The traditional Hungarian wedding ceremony features brightly burning candles, so it is quite likely that the song may be children's own playful reflection of this custom. For Kati, the song brings to mind beautiful memories of the many groups of children with whom she has shared this song over the years.

A circle, or ring game accompanies the song. One child is the "candle" in the center of the circle. When the children blow the candle out at the end of the song, he or she crouches down and then selects the next "candle."

Teaching Suggestions and Extensions

1. Sing the song in a circle, adding the following movements:

MM	1-4	Wave hands up and down (like the flickering of a candle flame)
MM	5-6	Bend head (flame) down low
MM	7-8	Stoop down, raise bottoms up

   Meanwhile, one child in the center moves freely about, blowing the candles out at the end of the song.

2. Discuss with children the familiar customs and seasonal events when candles are lit: religious functions, Birthdays, Christmas, Chanukah, Divali, for example.

3. Listen to recorded works by Kodaly (for example, the *Hary Janos Suite* or *The Peacock Variations*) and Bartok (for example, from the *Microkosmos* collection for piano) in order to taste the flavor of Hungarian folk melodies.

Ég a Gyertya

Translation by
Katalin Forrai

Traditional

Ég   a   gyer - tya   ég,   el   ne   a - lud - jék,

A - ki   lán - got   lát - ni   a - kar   mind   le - gug - gol - jék.

Translation
The candleleight is burning
I wish it kept on burning.
All that want to see the flame
Should crouch down.

Japan

 Cultural Information

Known as "the land of the rising sun," the small yet densely populated country of Japan lies northeast of China and east of Korea. Its four main islands (out of over 3,000 islands) include Hokkaido, Honshu, Kyushu, and Shikoku. Nearly 75 percent of the country is mountainous terrain, with nearly fifty active volcanoes and numerous earthquake faults. The most famous mountain, symbolic of Japanese culture, is Mt. Fuji, the dormant volcano which rises in the Tokyo skyline.

The Japanese are a homogenous people. While Japanese culture has been historically influenced by the Chinese and Koreans, and later by western cultures, the ethnic identity of the people has remained Japanese. The retention of Japanese as the national language reflects the unity of the people, despite the extent to which young and professional people study and use English. Religious practices also reflect commonality, with Buddhism being practiced by 75% of the population. Shinto, the former state religion (famous for temples with red symbolic statues) is often practiced simultaneously with Buddhism.

Japanese traditional arts reflect a sensitivity to beauty and nature. During the eighteenth and nineteenth centuries, many Japanese art forms were brought to their fullest development, including Kabuki theatre, Ukiyo-e woodblock print art, and forms of architecture and landscape design. Traditional folksongs of Japan, called *minyo*, are preserved through concerts, recordings, and contests that emphasize vocal skill and improvisatory ability. Seasonal celebrations at the new year, in summer (particularly the Bon Odori of August), spring planting and autumn harvest, show the strong connection which the modern Japanese still maintain to their religious and agrarian traditions. Drumming ensembles and folk dancing constitute important musical events which attract many Japanese—as audiences, if not participants. Instruments like the *koto* (a thirteen-string plucked zither) and the *shamisen* (a three-string plucked lute) continue to be studied by young people, with their repertoires preserved by master musicians and "national treasures."

About the Song: Toryanse

According to Sumio Gotoda, "Toryanse" is an old song known to the Japanese long before the Meiji era (1868-1912). In ancient times, there were many barriers to travelers, called *seki-sho*, at which officers would interrogate them as to their destinations and purposes for traveling. This singing game may have originated from the seki-sho dialogues.

The song's melody is felt in the rather typical Japanese duple meter. It is set in a hexatonic scale: c d eb f g ab c' that can be seen as two subsets—(d) f g ab c and c d eb g—that overlap yet function as separate modes. As can be expected, the singing game includes the formation of a barrier or gate, through which children may pass to continue on their travels to the Tenjin (Shinto) shrine.

Teaching Suggestions and Extensions

1. Sing the scale for the song, ascending and descending, twice as fast, twice as slow, "silently" and aloud (on cue, such as the sound of a hand-clap). In this way, the young singers will become vocally acquainted with the six pitches used in the melody.

2. Play the game that accompanies the song. Two children hold hands, making an arch that functions as a gate (as in "London Bridge"). Other children pass under the arch (through the gate) repeatedly, while singing the song. At the end of the song, the two children drop their hands, catching the child who is passing through the gate. The song begins again with new gatekeepers.

3. Discuss the historical origin of the song, describing the seki-sho system. Give the translation of the text, noting that the Tenjin shrine is a place to which people would travel to pay tribute to their ancestors, to pray for good fortune, and to purchase small charms to place in their homes.

Toryanse

Translation by
Sumio Gotoda

Traditional

To - ryan se, to - rya - n se, ko - ko wa, do - ko no ho - so - mi - chi ja?

Ten - jin - sa - ma no ho - sa - mi - chi ja. Cho - tto to - shi - te

ku - da - sha - n se? Go - yoo no na - i mo - no to - sha se - nu

Ko - no - ko no na - na - tsu no O - i - wa - i ni,

O - fu - da o o - sa - me ne ma - i - ri ma - su. I - ki wa

yo - i, yo - i, ka - e - ri wa ko - wa - i ko - wa - i

na - ga - ra - mo to - rya - n se to - rya - n se.

Translation
Please, pass through this lane.
Where does this lane lead?
It leads to the Tenjin shrine.
Please, let me go through it.
Have you anything for the shrine?
This is a gala day for my daughter of seven.
I wish to get a charm from the shrine.
Please, pass through, but
On your way back, you'll have trouble.
Being afraid, I would still go through.

Korea

 Cultural Information

Korea occupies a peninsula in northeast Asia that extends from the mainland out into the Sea of Japan. South Korea and North Korea became politically separated at the end of World War II. These predominantly mountainous countries are also two of the world's most densely populated countries.

Koreans are an ethnically homogenous people whose common heritage dates back to the seventh century. Korea's homogeneity is reflected in its common language, religion, and culture. The Korean alphabet, *hangul*, is believed to be the first phonetic alphabet in East Asia—others were based on pictographic characters. Confucianism, the official religion, and Buddhism are practiced by a majority of Koreans; about 28% are Christian or followers of *Chundo Kyo*, a nationalistic religion which combines the elements of Confucianism, Taoism, and Buddhism. Korea's rich artistic and cultural heritage has been strongly influenced by Buddhism brought from China. The influence of Buddhism was particularly strong from the 7th to the 12th century, and is evident in the *celadon* ceramics housed in temples, palaces and monasteries.

Musical practice reflects the Korean desire for homogeneity and the assimilation of musical ideas from the West. While the National Classical Music Institute performs court music at ceremonies at the Confucian and Royal Ancestors' Shrine, most middle-class families encourage their children to learn piano and violin. Traditional songs are still remembered by the elderly, and there is government support for efforts to preserve these songs, as well as genres of instrumental music. Chief among the traditional instruments of Korea are the *kayakeum* and *komungo*, long floor zithers, and the *changgo*-an hourglass drum with a wooden body, and numerous barrel drums.

About the Song: Arirang

There is perhaps no traditional Korean song more frequently performed by children's choirs and school bands and orchestras than "Arirang." It is performed (as it was traditionally evolved) as a monophonic melody, in canon, and in multiple parts, as befitting of the ensemble. Like many of Korea's traditional songs, "Arirang" has the feel of a triple meter and utilizes the pitches of the pentatonic scale. Like many Koreans, Sung-Hol Lee came to know this song at an early age—just as one learns language and cultural customs; it is pervasive throughout Korea.

 Teaching Suggestions and Extensions

1. While singing the song, conduct a three-beat pattern. Later, patsch the ♩ ♪ when it occurs; try also the ♪ ♩ and ♩ ♩ ♩ rhythms as they occur.

2. Sing the song as a canon, allowing a second group to enter one measure after the first group. For more sophisticated singers, attempt to sing a four-part canon, each entering one measure after the last.

3. Discuss the reference to "Arirang" as an idyllic place, in the colorful and flowerful hills. Examine photographs of Korea to discover the very real existence of hills and mountains, and to determine what kinds of wildflowers exist there.

Arirang

Translation by
Sung-Hol Lee

Traditional

Translation
Arirang, arirang, arariyo,
Over the hills of Arirang.

1. Voices call me from far away.
   I must follow, I cannot stay.

2. Years have passed since I went away.
   Back to Arirang I'll go some day.

The Netherlands

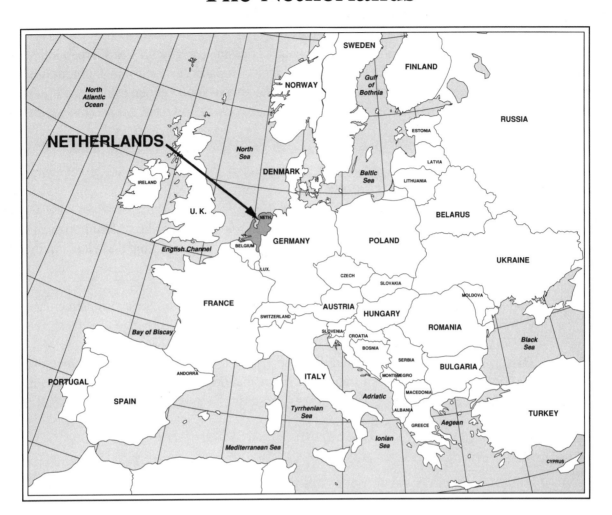

Cultural Information

Known also as "Holland" (after an historic region that is now part of the larger country), the Netherlands is a densely populated country in northeastern Europe. It is located on the North Sea, and is bordered by Germany and Belgium. "Neder" is Dutch for "low," and the Netherlands is one of the low countries, lying at sea level. (In fact, at high tide, approximately one-third of the Netherlands lies below sea level! Thus, the association of the country with dunes, dikes, and the regular pumping of excess water.)

The Dutch are an homogenous people with ancient origins in Germany, and some Celtic influence early on. Immigrants from Surinam, the South Moluccans, and Indonesia, along with foreign workers from the Mediterranean countries, have added to the populations. Dutch is the official language, although many speak English and German; Frisian, a separate Germanic language, is taught in the schools of the northern region of Friesland. Dutch society was once strictly divided among religious lines (Roman Catholicism and the Dutch Reformed Church), but today this separation is less rigid. Most of the population is employed in service-related, manufacturing or construction jobs, with smaller numbers in government and agriculture.

Folk music, although infrequently performed, is still evident in song, dance, and instrumental forms. Among the important idiophones still played are spoons, clappers, and rattles. Drums, including friction drums with holes in the skin through which a stick is drawn in and out, accompany dance music. Dulcimers, hurdy-gurdies, and bagpipes were once popular, but are no longer played. Evidence of clay whistles and a fiddle made from a wooden shoe add to the variety of musical timbres, but today, fiddles, button-key accordions, barrel organs, and brass bands are used to play for dances and gatherings.

About the Song: Komt Vrienden in Het Ronde

Dirk de Vreede explained that the song is about a craftsman who works to sharpen knives and scissors. This craftsman describes how he "earns a living," and then compares his job to the tailor, noting that he makes more in one hour than the tailor does in a day. The onomatapoeic sound of the grindstone ("ju ju ju") is the final sound of the refrain.

Teaching Suggestions and Extensions

1. Sing the harmonic minor scale as a warm-up to the song, in order to familiarize children with the pitches of the song. Sing the scale in a comfortable tempo, patting and clapping in a duple meter while singing. Then, sing it twice as fast.

2. Solfege the pitches l-si-l-m, adding hand levels or signs (or create a complementary gesture that corresponds with the pattern) each time the phrase occurs.

3. Discuss the manner in which traditional songs often refer to livelihoods and occupations of an earlier time. Collect a set of traditional songs that describe the ways of farmers, millers, and boatmen, for example.

Komt Vrienden In Het Ronde

Translation by
Dirk de Vreede and Peter Jense

Traditional

1. Komt vrien-den in het ron - de, min - naars van e - nen stiel; ik
2. De kleer-frik maakt ons kle - ren, voor acht stui-vers per dag: wil

zal u gaan ver - kon - den, hoe ik door't slij - pers wiel de
hij den loon ver - ma - ren, hij snijdt meer dan hij mag. Maar

kost ver-dien voor vrouw en kind, schoon blook-ge-steld aan weer en wind, ter -
ik met mij - ne slij - pers-steen, ik win meer op een uur al - leen

lie - re - lom ter - la! van links - om, rechts - om draait mij - ne steen door het

roe - ren van mijn been, ju, ju, ju, ju, ju, ju, ju, ju.

Translation

1. Dear friends come in the circle,
   Lovers of my profession.
   I will tell you how I sharpen my grindstone
   Earning my living for my wife and child
   Working in the open air.

2. The tailor makes clothes for us,
   For eight pennies per day.
   If he wants to increase his earnings,
   He cuts more cloth.
   But, I with my sharpened wheel,
   Earn more in an hour (than the tailor)
   does in a day.

Refrain:
From left to right turns my grindstone
as I move my legs.

New Zealand: Maori

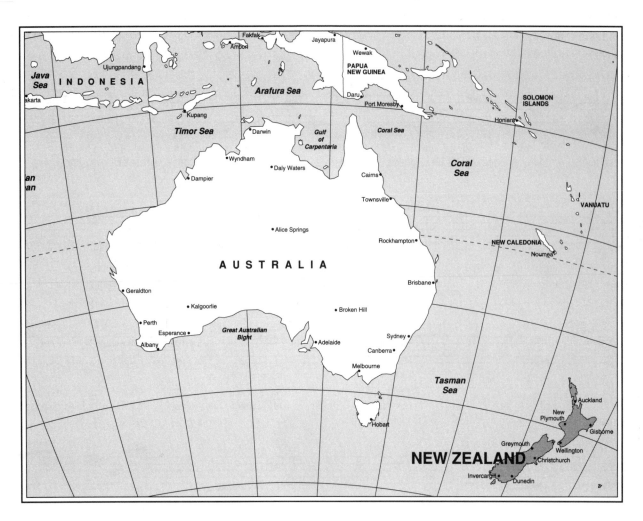

Cultural Information

The islands now called New Zealand were first settled by Polynesians, who became Maori people and named the islands Aotearoa. European settlement began after Captain James Cook surveyed the coastline in the 1770s. In 1840 the Treaty of Waitangi was signed between the British Crown and the Maori tribes, but while the Treaty granted civil rights equally to all, the Maori and English versions of the Treaty differed in significant ways. The Maori, for example, had no word for land ownership, and believed they were granting to Europeans the right to use the land, not the right to own it. Difficulties between the two cultures persisted, including wars, the prohibition of the Maori language in schools, and the attempted destruction of many aspects of traditional Maori culture, including musical instruments.

In 1984 the Maori version of the Treaty was officially recognized by the New Zealand Government as part of a move to establish New Zealand/Aotearoa as a bicultural/multicultural nation. While many other cultures are present within the social mix - including those of other Pacific Islands -- it is recognized that the Maori people, as the *tangata whenua* (the people of the land) have a special place.

A cultural revival has taken place among the Maori for much of the twentieth century. Tribal cultural groups have sought to preserve and renew the expression of the Maori in song and dance, using Maori texts, composed or borrowed tunes, and European harmony. To the Maori people, Music is less a separate "art-form" than an expression of the spiritual side of life. It must be linked to an occasion of some kind -- a formal welcome, or the giving of a speech, or a special performance. Singing is usually accompanied by guitar and by movement of some type, and performers are encouraged to add improvised harmony after the first verse.

In the last twenty years young urban Maori have found a way of expressing their cultural identity through Maori rock music.

Contributed by John Drummond, University of Otago, New Zealand

About the Song: Kia Kaha, Kia Toa E!

"Kia Kaha, Kia Toa E!" is a song of the Maori people of New Zealand. Stuart Manins learned the song from Keri Kaa, the head of the department of Maori Studies at Wellington Teachers College. He was very much an adult when he learned the song, as he began to explore for himself the music and culture of New Zealand's first people. Its message is clear: to be strong and courageous, and to follow the path to which you have been guided. With the blessings of the Maori, Stuart frequently uses this song as a musical means of bidding farewell to friends—at an educational conference, or after a teaching session with children.

Teaching Suggestions and Extensions

1. While singing the song, keep a patsch-clap-clap ostinato. The song invokes a swaying feeling, too, to the left or right, once every three beats.

2. Using two rhythm sticks, children may sit in a circle on the floor and tap this pattern while singing:

| tap-floor | tap sticks together | tap sticks together |

3. In pairs facing one another, children may tap this pattern while singing:

| tap-floor | tap sticks together | tap partner's sticks |

4. Discuss the meaning of the song. Note that its particular occasion for performance is at the departure of family members or friends from the home, just as other songs are specific for welcoming them.

Kia Kaha, kia toa e!

Translation by
Stuart Manins

Traditional

Hae - re ha - e - re ra kia ka ka - ha

ki - a to - a e ki te wne -

nu - a i te ta - ha o te to -

nga e wha - ka - ria nei. _____

Hae - re hae - re ha - e - re - ra.

Translation
Farewell, go with strength and courage
To that chosen direction (south)
Illuminated for you.

Portugal

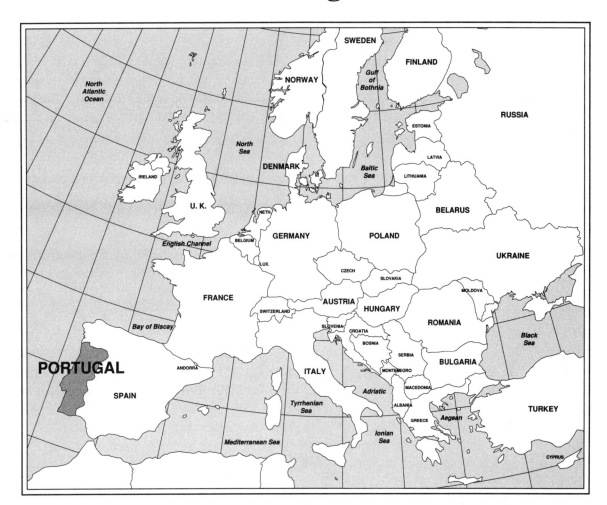

 Cultural Information

One of the oldest countries in Europe, Portugal's name is thought to be derived from the Roman settlement of Portus Cale on the Atlantic Ocean. Its only neighbor is Spain; together, the two countries form the Iberian Peninsula.

Portugal is one of Europe's most homogenous populations. The only sizable minority is the nearly 100,000 black colonial refugees from the former Portuguese African colonies. Portuguese, one of the five Romance languages, is the official language, and Roman Catholicism is the professed faith of 97 percent of the population.

Portugal's folk music and dance traditions include ornate and melismatic singing and instrumental performance (especially in the remote mountainous regions, and on the islands), and African rhythms, forms, and instruments. Song styles such as the *guineos* and *negros* are examples of African genres placed in a European context, and feature responsorial forms and hemiola shifts to 3/4 within a 6/8 meter. Portugal is also known for its lyrical songs and *Fado*, the urban vocal music of cafes, cabarets and night clubs. Fado typically contains some improvised sections in strophic form, and is accompanied by I, IV, and V7 chords on the viola (a four- or five-string guitar) and the *guitarra portuguesta* (a long-necked lute). The children's songs of Portugal are frequently diatonic or pentatonic, their melodies moving stepwise are in the tones of a triad.

About the Song: Indo Eu

"Indo Eu" has been popular since at least the 1920s among adolescent boys and girls. Fernanda Prim was about 7 or 8 years old when she learned this song at school, but it is often transmitted by mothers to children, or from child to child on the street. The melody conjures up for Fernanda the many times she has sung the song as a child and teacher of children: at school programs, festivals, and folk dances. "Ai Jesus!" is an exclamation similar to "Oh my goodness," and means here "Help! I am falling down."

Teaching Suggestions and Extensions

1. Explain that "Viseu" is a small city in Portugal, that "ora zus, truz, truz" are semantically meaningless syllables, and "arreda!" means "get back."

2. Play the singing game:

MM 1-2	Join hands in a circle, and step to the right. (4 counts)
MM 3	Continue to step to the right. (2 counts)
MM 4	Stop, put hands on head, and sit in a squatting position. (2 counts)
MM 5	Turn to a neighbor, and clap on "zus truz truz." (2 counts)
MM 6	Turn to another neighbor, and clap on "zas tras tras." (2 counts)
MM 7-8	Join hands, step to the center of the circle, and then back out again. (4 counts)

Indo eu

Translation by
Fernanda Prim

Traditional

In - do eu in - do eu a ca - min - ho de Vi - seu

En - con - trai o meu a - mor ai Je - sus que la vou eu

O - ra zuz, truz truz, o - ra zaz, traz traz

O - ra che - ga che - ga che - ga o - ra 'rre - da la p'ra traz

Translation
When I was going, when I was going
In my way to Viseu,
I met my love
Oh my goodness! I fall down.

Ora zus, truz, truz
Ora zas, tras tras
Ora come, come, come
Ora move back, back, back

Taiwan

 Cultural Information

Taiwan is a large island located 115 miles from the southeastern coast of China. Known as the Republic of China (ROC), Taiwan is one of the world's leading trade economies. Benefiting from its competent labor force, Taiwan has become a leading producer of electronics, textiles, plastics, and toys.

The majority of the Taiwanese descended from Chinese immigrants in the eighteenth and nineteenth centuries. Like the great majority of the population of mainland China, they are members of the Han ethnic culture. Most of the population speaks Fukien, the dialect of Fujian province of southeastern China. About 15 percent are "mainlanders" who arrived more recently to Taiwan in China, to escape communist rule from 1949 onward. A small group of non-Chinese aborigines, possibly descended from Indonesian origin, live in the central highlands. Most Taiwanese live in the densely populated cities, including Taipei, the capitol city.

Taiwan views itself as the major center of Chinese traditional art, literature, and music. The National Palace Museum is known for its collection of bronzes and Chinese paintings. The traditional forms of Chinese opera and *Yuan* drama are frequently performed, and Chinese classical arts such as calligraphy are preserved and encouraged through education. Music plays an integral part of Taiwanese life, as it does among the Han Chinese on China's mainland, where music has been traditionally employed for planting, harvesting, fishing and hunting, along with its use in temples and temple yards for religious purposes. Music and dance is prominent at weddings and New Year's celebrations, from *luogu* drum-and-gong ensembles to the sounds of "silk" instruments like the *zheng* (a sixteen- or seventeen-string zither), *pipa* (a pear-shaped lute), and *erhu* (a two-stringed fiddle).

About the Song: Tioo Bai Lo Ho

Jane Wang selected this song as an example of Taiwanese dialect and singing style. The melody utilizes a pentatonic scale, s-l-d-r-m (c-d-f-g-a), with the addition of "ti" (e) just once (measure 11) as a melodic ornament. A few grace notes and several dotted rhythms give the melody greater intricacy. The text refers to rural life concentrated on the collection of food from the earth (roots) and fish from the sea. Cecilia Wang provided the romanization of the Chinese characters, and Margaret Tse provided a basic translation of the text.

 Teaching Suggestions and Extensions

1. Sing the pentatonic scale, s-l-d-r-m that forms the basis of the melody, ascending and descending at a moderate tempo. On cue, sing silently certain designated pitches (so or la, for example), while continuing to keep the same tempo up and down the scale. Add "ti."

2. Play the melody on recorders, and add a rhythmic percussion ostinato to accompany the melody. (WB is woodblock, DR is a drum [played with hard mallets] and BL is a bell or triangle)

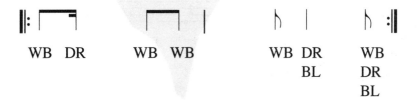

WB	DR	WB	WB	WB	DR	WB
					BL	DR
						BL

3. Discuss the facets of rural life, rapidly fading from Taiwan, China, and elsewhere, where the daily events are centered on the collection and preparation of meals. Collect other songs that describe this pre-industrial lifestyle.

Tioo Bai lo Ho

Transliteration Cecilia Wang
Translation by Margaret Tse

Traditional

Ti - o - o   Bai lo Ho   A Gong A Gia Di Tau Bai __ Gu __   Or

Gu   A   Gu   Gu   A   Gu   Gu   De   Ju   Bai __   Shaun Liu   Guor

I   Ya Hei   Do   Jin   Jian   Qu   Bi,   A   Gong A   Bai   Ju   Guan

A   Ma __   Bai   Ju   Jua   Nun   E __   Shu   Pa   Long   Pa   Dian

I   Yo He   Do   Lon   Don   Chi   Don   Chian   Ha   Ha   Ha   Ha   Ha   Ha.

Translation
The sky is dark, It wants to rain.
Grandpa lifts his hoe to dig up taro roots.
Hoe, ah, hoe. Hoe, ah, Hoe. Find a fish, too.
We have fun collecting food for our meal.
Grandpa wants to cook his meal with salt.
Grandma wants to cook her meal without salt.
The two of them talk and tug the cooking pot until it breaks.
Ha, Ha, Ha: Ha, Ha, Ha!

Uganda

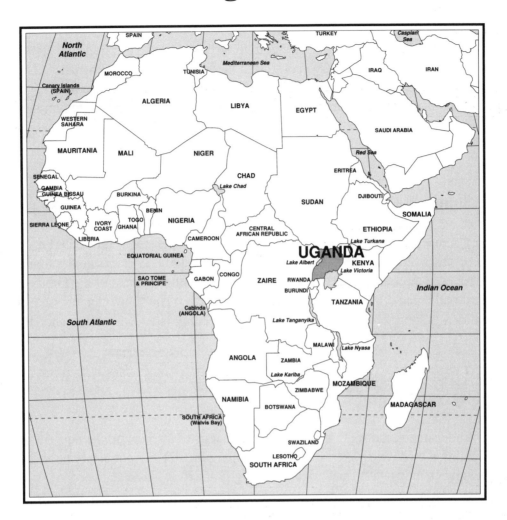

Cultural Information

Uganda is a landlocked country in the equatorial region of eastern Africa. Bordered by Sudan, Zaire, Rwanda, Tanzania, Kenya, and the scenic Lake Victoria, Uganda claims lakes as nearly one-fifth of its territory. Its volcanic and snow-capped mountains are rich repositories of copper and cobalt, while its lowlands allow for the production of coffee, cotton, and tea.

As it is throughout the countries of Africa, ethnic identification is important to the people of Uganda. Some groups have long histories, while others were formed in the British colonial period of the last few centuries. Some groups are ruled by kings, while others are more egalitarian societies. Among the major ethnic groups are the Nyoro, Ganda, Bakiga, Gisu, Nubian, Baganda, Acholi, Lani, and Karamojong. Although Swahili and Luganda are commonly spoken, English is the official language of Uganda. Being challenged by turbulent decades of political oppression (one very dark period was the regime of Idi Amin) and issues of public health, Uganda is now involved in the slow process of rebuilding its economy and educational systems.

Music has many uses in Uganda: entertainment, enculturation and education, ceremonial or religious songs, songs of hunting and harvesting, and praise songs, among others. Drums, *enseege* gourds with beads (inside and netted outside), animal horns, and small bows and fiddles are played, but singing and dancing—often with body percussion—are the principal means of music-making among the people of Uganda.

Baganda Culture

The Baganda culture is a Bantu-based culture of East Africa. The Baganda are an agricultural people found mostly in central and southern Uganda. Their staple food is matooke bananas. One ruled by kings, clan membership is very important today among the Baganda, as it affects who you marry (preferably outside your clan) as well as the marriage traditions. Respect for one's elders is another important value of the Baganda people.

About the Song: Tuula Tuula Wakati

Sister Catherine Nakatudde, DM learned this song from Sister Theresa, DM at Narozali Primary School when she was 7 years old. "Tuula Tuula Wakati" teaches children to celebrate life together. It is grounded in the Baganda belief in the interconnection of the individual with members of the family and the community at large, and mirrors the pan-African view of "the circle of life." The song may at first seem to resemble the melody of children's songs elsewhere, but when the drumming is added, the Baganda flavor is undeniable.

Teaching Suggestions and Extensions

1. While singing the song, patsch the subdivisions of the beat on the lap. At a later time, offer children these two patterns to patsch, tapping the left or right hand on the left or right leg, while chanting "left" and "right," or "high" and "low" as designated

2. Play the ostinati patterns (called *ngoma*, or drum patterns) on high and low drums, alternating between them, or play them on two drums. Add a shaker (called *enseege* in Luganda) for this rhythm:

3. Form a circle and play the game. Children hold hands and step to the right while singing. During the first line, the children look around the circle at their friends. During the second line, the chosen child chooses a partner and they both dance together during the third line. Group clapping is added on the fourth line. The last two phrases are often sung by the two children dancing in the middle. One child dances freely in the middle of the circle, and on "Gze nnonze," chooses a partner to dance with in the middle. [Please note that "ca-te," lines 5 and 6, is a person's name; substitute the name of the child that is chosen as a dancing partner.]

4. Discuss the meaning of "the circle of life" to the Baganda people of Uganda who sing this song, and to Africans at large.

Mutubaruke Emihanda

Translation by
Sister Justine Tumushabe, DM

Traditional

Mu - tu - ba - ru - ke ___ emi - han - da yaan - yu, ___ eyim - wa - ra -

ba - mu ___ Ok - wii - ja ha - nu. ___ Mu - tu - ba -
Ku - twaa - hu -

rii - re ___ ngu ni mwen - da kwi - ija, ___ Twa - she - me -

D.C. al Fine   ⊕ *Coda*

re - rwa ___ o - bu - ta ga - mbwa ___ Mu - tu ba   ha - nu. ___

Translation
When we heard that you wanted to visit,
We were extremely happy,
In a way we cannot say in words.

Bakiga Culture

The Bakiga people of Uganda are bound together by their common language, Rukiga. Like other ethnic-cultural groups of Uganda, they pay great respect to their elders, taking care of them and heeding their advice. The elders often give their wisdom in the form of proverbs, stories, and songs. The Bakiga are hospitable people, welcoming their fellow Ugandans to their community and homes with a bowl of porridge (*obushera*) made from home-grown sorghum and millet. In recent years, the overpopulation of Bakiga villages has resulted in the migration of some to new territories where fertile fields are open for planting and farming is less competitive.

About the Song: Matabaruke Emihanda

As her older sisters sang "Matabaruke Emihanda" at home, Sister Justine B.V. Tumushabe, DM learned the song, too. She was 5 years old. The song is a welcoming of visitors into the home, and an acknowledgement of the hardships they may have encountered on their journey. The singing is typically accompanied by hand-clapping, swaying, and *ebinzino* dancing.

Teaching Suggestions and Extentions

1. Using first patching on the lap, and then conga drums to substitute for Bakiga engoma drums, try these patterns:

and

2. A shaker, called a *kakyeenkye*, can be used to play these alternating patterns:

3. Sing while playing the percussion parts. Without partners, without a circle or line formation, move freely to rhythm and spirit of the music.

4. Use the song to welcome visitors to the classroom or school, inviting them to join in by clapping, swaying, and dancing. The spirit of the singing should relay much happiness.

Tuula Tuula Wakati

Translation by
Sister Catherine Nakatudde, DM

Traditional

Tuu - la   Tuu - la   wa - ka - ti   Nǵo   tun - u - li - raa   baa   na

Go - lo - ko - ka - wo   man - gu   oj   je   ol - lon   de   oyo   gwo - lon - ze____

____   Mwem-bi   mud - de   wa - ka - ti   nga   mu - zi - na   Ness' - an - yu

Tu - na - ku - ba   mu   Nga - lo   ol - w'ess - an - yu - lya - ffe._____

Nze   nnon - ze   ca - te,   maa - ma,   Bwe   Bu - la - mu   Bwan - ge

nze   nnon - ze   ca - te,   maa - ma,   er - a   gw'en - sii - mye.

Translation

Sit down in the middle of the circle and gaze at the children, your friends.
Get up quickly and choose one of them.
Both of you go in the middle of the circle while dancing with joy.
We shall clap because of happiness.
I have chosen Cate, because I love her.
I have chosen Cate because I have favored her.

The United States

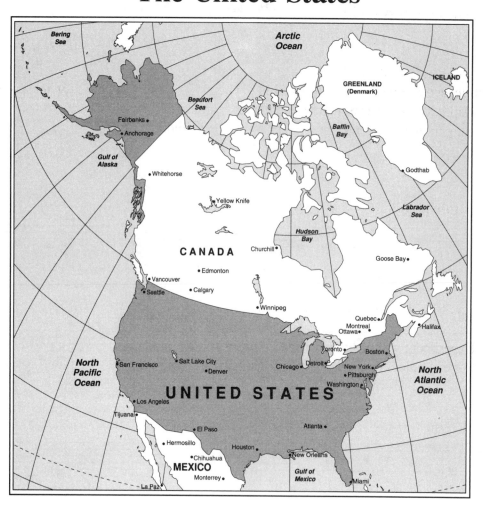

 ## Cultural Information

The United States (the U.S., the United States of America, or the U.S.A.) is located in the middle of the North American continent, with Canada and Mexico as northern and southern neighbors, respectively. It comprises at least four basic geographic (and cultural) regions: the eastern coast (including New York, Boston, and Washington, D.C.), the south (from the tobacco states of North and South Carolina, and from Florida to Texas), the midwest (including the hub-city of Chicago), and the west (including the Rocky mountains, the desert states of Arizona and New Mexico, and the west coast cities of Los Angeles, San Francisco, and Seattle).

The population of the United States represents a heritage of diverse world cultures. The indigenous people, the Native American Indians, were the country's first inhabitants until European colonization that began in the early sixteenth century. Currently, while many citizens reflect European heritages, ethnic groups once termed minority are making sizable population gains. About 12 percent of the population is classified African-American, while the Hispanic population stands at about 8 percent, and Asians at 4 percent.

American dance and music reflects the diversity of the United States. Much of the population listens to popular music, including rock and rap, that is made accessible by the large recording industry. In the classical vein, there is the gamut of orchestral, choral, and opera productions from which to choose, along with music that accompanies ballet and modern dance performances. Long-standing American folk traditions include the folk-songs and instrumental music of Anglo-Americans including play party songs, fiddle tunes, and ballads, the cowboy songs of the west, and the highly rhythmic sacred and secular music of African-Americans—from the blues to gospel."

About the Song: Simple Gifts

    "Simple Gifts" is a well-known traditional song, originating from the Shaker religious communities once active in Kentucky in the eighteenth and nineteenth centuries. The sentiment of simplicity was at the core of the philosophy of the Shakers, who lived devout lives centered on the principles of peace, communal sharing and simplicity. Victoria Schultz remembered learning this song as a child in her elementary school music classes, and now teaches the song to her own schoolchildren.

 Teaching Suggestions and Extensions

1. Sing the song lightly tapping the pulse ♩ and later, subdivisions of the pulse (♪♪).

    Combine the two into a basic ostinato for the hand drum: ♩ ♪♪ .

2. Experiment with singing selected phrases solo, in small groups, and as a full ensemble. For example, measures 1 and 2 might be sung solo, measures 3 and 4 as a duet, and measures 5-8 as a full ensemble piece.

3. Discuss the meaning of the text, and the importance of simple things in life (healthy meals, friends, a loving family) that make for a good life.

Simple Gifts

Traditional

'Tis the gift to be sim - ple, 'tis the gift to be free, 'Tis the

gift to come down where we ought to be. And when we find our - selves in the

place just right, 'Twill be in the val - ley of love and de - light. When true sim -

pli - ci - ty is gained, To bow and to bend we shan't be a - shamed. To

turn, turn will be our de - light, Till by turn - ing, turn - ing we come 'round right.

Yiddish

Cultural Information

Spoken by 11 million Jews on the eve of World War II, Yiddish is the vernacular language of relatively few contemporary Jews. Yiddish vocabulary is a fusion of German, Hebrew-Aramaic, Romance, and Slavic terms; a blend of linguistic contributions tracing European regions in which Jews have lived from the sixth century to the present.

Yiddish folklore which Jewish immigrants brought to the United States in the early twentieth century has enriched American culture. In 1978, Polish-born American writer Isaac Bashevis Singer won the Nobel Prize in literature for his narrative work written in Yiddish. Tales of Tevye, The Dairyman and his Daughters, the Yiddish stories of Ukrainian-born American writer, Sholom Alcheim (nee Solomon Rabinowitch), were adapted in the Broadway musical, *Fiddler on the Roof*. The Yiddish expressions *shlep, kvetch, khutspa, bagel, shlemiel*, and *shlimazel* have found common usage in American vernacular.

About the song: Sheyn Bin Ikh, Sheyn

"Sheyn Bin Ikh, Sheyn" is an example of a song that little girls might have sung as they acted out the traditional Jewish wedding. These bride-and-groom games were the mimetic expression of what was perhaps the most important event in the Jewish life cycle. A wedding match (*shidukh*, plural *shidukhim*) with a rabbinical scholar was considered most fortuitous. Supporting a husband in his study of the *Torah* (Hebrew Scriptures) was an honored vocation for a wife.

The relationship of Yiddish to German is apparent in the title of the song, although Yiddish is sometimes pronounced differently from German. The expression for "I am" is "ich bin" in German and "ikh bin" in Yiddish.

Miriam Dvorin Spross heard Yiddish spoken by her parents, grandparents, aunts and uncles. Unlike her mother who attended *kindershul* where Yiddish was taught, Miriam attended Hebrew school. Since Yiddish is written in Hebrew characters, learning to read Yiddish was easy for Miriam. The song is found in *Jewish Folk Songs in Yiddish and English* by Ruth Rubin, a songbook Miriam gave her maternal *bubbe* (grandmother) with the inscription, "For my grandmother, with whom I share a love for the music and culture of the Jewish People." The song is also found in Ruth Rubin's *Voices of a People: The Story of Yiddish Folksong*.

Teaching Suggestions and Extensions

1. Several phrases of the song are repeated. Sing these while describing the rise and fall of the pitches with corresponding hand motions.

MM	1-2, 9-10	s-f-m-s
MM	17-18, 19-20	s-m-d-s-m
MM	25-26, 27-28, 29-30	s-f-m-r-d

2. Create a "patschen" game (e.g. "Miss Mary Mack") based on eighth notes that repeats every measure or every two measures. Sing the song and perform the pattern, accelerating the tempo so that the song becomes a "tongue twister."

3. Discuss the custom of match-making in Eastern European Jewish culture with reference to the centrality of this theme in *Fiddler on the Roof*. How are marriages made in various cultures? When marriages are arranged, who does the arranging?

4. Look for more Yiddish stories and songs in:
   Aleichem, Sholom. *The Old Country*. Trans. Julius and Frances Butwin.
     New York: Crown Publishers, Inc., 1946.
   Dvorin, Miriam. *Grandma Soup: Yiddish Songs,* audiocassette. Vida, OR:
     Pacific Cascade Records, 1983.
   Rubin, Ruth. *Jewish Folk Songs in Yiddish and English*. New York:
     Oak Publications, 1965.
   Rubin, Ruth. *Voices of a People: The Story of Yiddish Folk Song*.
     Philadelphia: The Jewish Publication Society of America, 1979.
   Singer, Isaac Bashevis. *Stories for Children*. New York Farrar/Straus/Giroux, 1985.

YIDDISH PRONUNCIATION

	as in		as in		as in
a	far	u	full	sh	fish
e	bed	ay	why	ts	lets
i	is	ey	they	y	yes
o	so	oy	boy	kh	li-**kh**a-yim!

Sheyn Bin Ich, Sheyn

Translation by
Miriam Dvoria

Traditional

Sheyn bin ich sheyn. Sheyn iz oych mayn no - men. Redt men mir shi -

du - chim mit groy - se ra - bo - nim. Ra - bo - ni - she toy - re

iz doch zey - er groys, _ Bin ich bay mayn ma - men a lich - ti - ge royz.

A sheyn mey-de - le bin ich, Bloy - e ze-ke-lech trog ich, Gelt in di ta - shn,

Vayn in di fla - shn, Med in di kri - ge lech, kind - er in di vi - ge - lech,

Shray - en vi di tsi - ge - lech: Meh, Meh, Meh. _____

Translation

Pretty am I, so pretty,
Pretty too, is my name,
Wedding matches only of rabbis
    come my way.
Torah learning is indeed very great,
I am my mother's bright rose.

A pretty maid am I, am I,
Blue socks do I wear, wear,
Money in the purses, wine in the
    bottles,
Mead in the little pitchers, children
    in the little cradles,
Cry like little kids: ma, ma, ma.

Bibliography

Amoaku, W. Komla. *African Songs and Rhythms for Children.* New York: Schott, 1986.

Bronner, Simon J., *American Children's Folklore: A Book of Rhymes, Games, Jokes, Stories, Beliefs and Camp Legends.* Little Rock, AR: August House, 1988.

Campbell, Patricia Shehan, Ellen McCullough-Brabson. *Roots and Branches.* Danbury, Ct: World Music Press, 1994.

East Helen. T*he Singing Sack: Twenty-eight Song-Stories from Around the World.* London: A & C Black, 1989.

Ebinger, Virgina Nylander, Ninez. *Spanish Songs, Games, and Stories of Childhood.* Santa Fe, NM: Sunstone Press, 1993.

Fukuda, Hanako. *Favorite Songs of Japanese Children.* Van Nuys, CA: Alfred, 1964.

Fulton, Eleanor and Pat Smith. *Let's Slice the Ice.* St. Louis: Magnamusic-Baton, 1978.

Fuoco-Lawson. *Gloria, Street Games.* London: Schott, 1992.

Jones, Bessie and Bess Lomax Hawes. *Step It Down: Games, Plays, Songs & Stories from the Afro-American Heritage.* Athens, GA: University of Georgia Press, 1972.

Opie, Peter and Iona Opie. *The Singing Game.* Oxford: Oxford University Press, 1988.

Seeger, Ruth Crawford. *American Folk Songs for Children.* New York: Doubleday, 1975.